T0210074

Letters
from the
Prairies

CHANSOO KIM, M.D.

authorHOUSE®

AuthorHouse™
1663 Liberty Drive
Bloomington, IN 47403
www.authorhouse.com
Phone: 1 (800) 839-8640

Published by AuthorHouse 07/03/2019

ISBN: 978-1-7283-1703-8 (sc)
ISBN: 978-1-7283-1702-1 (e)

Library of Congress Control Number: 2019908506

Print information available on the last page.

This book is printed on acid-free paper.

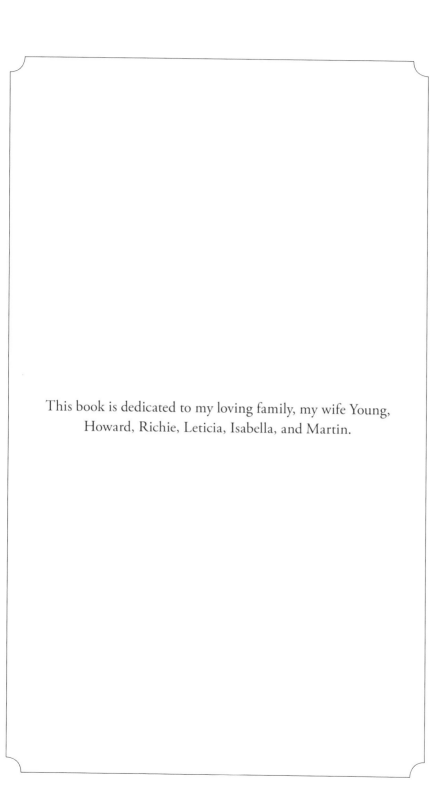

This book is dedicated to my loving family, my wife Young, Howard, Richie, Leticia, Isabella, and Martin.

Contents

Preface

"Letters from Prairies" comes as a sequel to my first book, "Just My Two Cents" which was published in 2012 by Authorhouse. This book follows the intents and purposes of my first book..

I am well aware that my voice is freeble and hardly audible like "a voice in the wilderness". Yet, I believe that I leave behind my footprints on the Prairies that I have traversed thus far.

Almost all my articles in this book were published in The State Journal-Register, also called "Lincoln Newspaper". I did not hesitate to venture my humble opinions on the vast number of subjects ranging from current medical issues to "hot button" social issues..

At the end of my book, I added "Life and Legacy of my mentor Howard A. Rusk, M.D. for the benefits of posterity. Dr. Rusk is called the Father of Rehabilitation Medicine. He was also the great benefactor of Korea. However, in my last year of training, he personally helped me to get the position of Associate Professor of PM&R, University of Hawaii Medical School Postgraduate Medical program in Okinawa. There I met my most unforgettable colleagues in my life, Drs. Neil L and Sarah Gault. Dr. NL Gault became the first Medical Director of University of Hawaii Medical School postgraduate program in Okinawa in 1967. His wife, Sarah Gault as a physiatrist was the founder of PM&R Department. I became her successor when they left the Islands. One of Dr. Gault's remarkable contributions to international medical education was the pivotal role he played as the University of Minnesota Medical school's first Visiting Professor to Seoul national Medical school. His family lived in Seoul in 1954 to 1961 to rebuild the medical education system there. This visit sparked the medical school's international collaboration. This partnership still continues to flourish today. Likewise, his Okinawa's post graduate program just celebrated the Golden Anniversary in 2017 as his tribute. Dr.

Gault received The Order of The Rising Sun from The Emperor Akihito in 1992 followed by honorary Alumnus of Seoul National University College of Medicine in 1994.

Lastly, my special thanks should go to then High Commisioner for his involvement in Rehab. workshops for local hospitals on Miyako and Yaeyama islands, 178 miles southwest Okinawa.

"Illegal" is just that

(State Journal-Register, May 26, 2012)

The political correctness virus strikes us again. Its madness is so insufferable that we all feel like being kicked in the teeth.

The PC crowd dare says that from now on, we should no longer call illegal immigrants as illegal aliens. Rather, we should address to them "foreign nationals." Otherwise, we are committing "a hate crime."

Their flaky reasoning is that "no human beings are illegal and the very word illegal is, therefore, a dehumanizing slur and should be by all means dropped." They go on to decry that the "I" word is as bad as the "N" word.

However, we live in the land of law, and if anyone, regardless of ethnic background, enters the country to live illegally or against the law, he is and should be declared an illegal alien and should be dealt with as such. Illegal by any other word is still illegal. Indeed, what would happen to us if we get rid of the word "illegal"? We will be living in hell with no need for the law. Now, it is so obvious that the relentless PC campaign is definitely getting out of control, taking up the mantel of the Orwellian thought police in the 21st century.

"Illegal" is just that (5/26/2012)

Comments;

(1) Dropping the illegal alien moniker is their attempt at humanizing their crime and becoming legal citizens unlike others who come here and follow the rule of law and become legal citizens through the current process.

(2) Right on target! The left changes to distort reality. For incidence, changing bum to homeless. This is a truly disservice to homeless but it promotes big government solutions.

(3) I agree with the author illegals get more benefits than honest Americans these days. Free housing, free medical care, free education, and free income tax breaks.

(4) It used to be "undocumented alien" like it was just a minor error in paperwork. Once on TV a protest I saw the protest leader complaining because the illegals couldn't even vote. In Mexico the police or army on mere suspicion can stop a person and make prove they are not in the country. If they can't, they are driven to the nearest border, beaten up and thrown out of the country.

I have the Brooklyn Bridge to sell

(Illinois Times, June 10, 2012)

Guestwork by Lew Prince (May 3-9/ Illinois Times) makes me wonder if we live in the same country. He talks as if the Buffet Rule were the right medicine, if not a panacea, for our worst financial crisis since the Great Depression. Lest we miss the forest for the trees, a brief review of the earth-shaking events the past few years certainly seems to be in order.

1) Early in 2010, President Obama established the National Commission on Fiscal Responsibility and Reform, which is hereafter known as the Bowles-Simpson Commission for Federal Deficit Reduction. On 12/1/2010, the Bowles-Simpson (bipartisan) Commission released its final and comprehensive report. But unfortunately their recommendations were rejected practically out of the hand.

2) In August, 2011, for the first time in U.S. history, Uncle Sam's credit rating was downgraded by Standard and Poor's to double A+ from triple A as the national debt continued to soar to an unsustainable level and the U.S. was, at the time, on the brink of default.

3) As usual, the buck was passed again to Congress and then its Super Committee (bipartisan). They also failed miserably to make a compromise for a deficit reduction plan, which is par for the course. Certainly, Washington has had plenty of opportunities in the past two years on matters of budget, taxes and federal debt to rise to the occasion as they did back in 1983, but has consistently failed to do so. All of a sudden, the Buffett Rule appears out of nowhere as a White Knight; yet, the Joint Committee on Taxation estimates the Buffett Rule would yield between $4 billion and $5 billion a year. According to Charles Krauthammer, a nationally known commentator, "If we collect Buffett tax for the next 250 years - a span longer than the life of the republic - it would not cover the Obama deficit for 2011 alone."

He continued to say that the Buffett Rule could be clever politics, as a sop to class warfare, but in terms of economics, it is worse than useless. Other pundits chimed in calling the Buffett Rule a "Buffett ruse." Recently, on May 3, 2012, Erskine Bowles (D) co-chairman of President Obama's deficit reduction commission said that "the U.S. faces the most predictable economic crisis." Again, according to Bowles, "100% of the tax revenue coming in to the Treasury in 2011 went right out the door to pay for mandatory spending such as Medicare, Medicaid and Social security, and to pay the interest on the country's massive $15.6 trillion national debt.

The train has left the station and we are now driving full speed ahead towards the edge of so called financial cliff. This grave fiscal crisis calls for bolder leadership now than ever before. As the cliche goes, "No gut, no glory and no pain, no gain." If Prince believes, as he does, that the Buffett Rule would go a long way towards our fiscal solvency, I have the Brooklyn Bridge for sale.

CTS a complex ailment

(State Journal-Register, July 25, 2012)

The State Journal-Register's July 16 Health section issued a warning that "wrist pain may be carpal tunnel syndrome." The whole issue of CTS is far more complex than it appears to be, like a "tip of an iceberg."

As we all know, CTS is caused by a host of medical conditions –– to name just a few of them, diabetes, rheumatoid arthritis, osteoarthritis, hypothyroidism, morbid obesity, amyloidosis, tenosynovitis, ganglion cyst and wrist fracture, etc. Vocational or occupational CTS is often seen among meat cutters, painters, carpenters, farmers and heavy equipment operators, particularly jackhammer operators.

On the other hand, avocational or recreational factors include gardening, baking, sewing, quilting, crocheting, cycling, musical instrument players and sign language.

It should be noted here that female gender with use of oral contraceptives is the strongest of risk factors. Furthermore, congenital and hereditary CTS also do occur.

Back in 1986, I had a rare opportunity to perform Electrodiagnostic study (EDX or EMG) on the former Oscar Mayer's 83 prospective job applicants as part of a pre-employment screening process. Surprisingly enough, 15-20 percent of those applicants were found to be positive for CTS. This survey points us to the fact that some of us may have exiting "asymptomatic" CTS, whether medical or otherwise. The combination of two or more risk factors makes the perfect storm for CTS.

Thus, the public should be shielded from misleading medical information that wrist pain may be carpal tunnel syndrome and that CTS is all work-related.

Petraeus affair is nothing new

(State Journal-Register, Dec 10, 2012)

Kathleen Parker in her recent commentary pens the David Petraeus affair as the American complex.

However, it is simply amusing the way she goes about the story of Petraeus' extramarital affair.

She just seems to be unaware of or conveniently forgetting the sex scandals of the late 1990s that rocked the nation and the world.

The women involved in the gross and sordid sex escapades had been called all kinds of degrading names, not just "ambitious, hormonally charged vixens," as Parker discreetly labels them.

If you recall, we were admonished at the time –– and polls concurred –– that adultery is none of our business, as it is a consensual sex between two adults. Rather, we should leave the matter up to the person involved and his spouse and family.

That was not the case with Adm. John Scudi. Because of adultery charges, he was forced to retire at a lower rank with a reduced pension. To add insult to injury, he was placed under a 30-day arrest in his quarters and eventually received a punitive letter of reprimand.

If Bill Clinton were allowed to run again for president, he would be easily re-elected. Talk about a double standard all you want. If Parker seriously brushes up on the sex scandals of the erstwhile famous politicians, she would realize that the Petraeus affair is no longer the American complex. It is what we call the new normal.

Consider health effects of sports

(State Journal-Register, Jan 5, 2013)

The Dec. 24 Health section's Heady Stuff deals with symptoms and signs of concussions in general, thus leaving much to be desired for important considerations of the late onset of subsequent chronic traumatic encephalopathy (CTE), which is a progressive neurodegenerative disease.

CTE occurs three times more frequently among professional football players. For example, Alzheimer's, dementia, Parkinson's disease and Amyotrophic Lateral Sclerosis –– also known as Lou Gehrig's disease –– the risk increased four times greater than the general population.

Sadly, the legendary Muhammad Ali suffers from Parkinson's syndrome. It's no wonder why 2,000 players are now suing the NFL, claiming that the league "downplays and misrepresents the issues and misled the players concerning the risks associated with concussions."

Of all notorious, yet much loved contact sports, such as football, ice hockey, boxing and wrestling, the worst culprit is boxing. Still, boxing is just as popular worldwide. Boxer's demential (Pugilistica Dementia) affects 15 to 20 percent of boxers.

The word pugilistica comes from the Latin root pugil for boxer. If you recall, some years back, the American Medical Association took its official stand against boxing solely for medical reasons. It is about time to seriously reconsider the AMA's recommendation.

Timbuktu

(State Journal-Register, Feb 18, 2013)

In English language, the word Timbuktu is figuratively used for "the most distance place available / or unknown place". For incidence, when someone asked, "Where is Charlie?", you would go like this, "He is somewhere in Timbuktu" After all, Timbuktu is the name of a town in central Mali, western Africa, near the Niger River and it is also otherwise known as Timboucton for French. Mali has been in the headline news since the beginning of the year 2013 when al-Qaida linked extremists had seized control of its northern half. But thanks to the French military's swift intervention, Timbuktu was finally liberated late last month. Now, Timbuktu has lost the Century-old notoriety of "being a far-away and outlandish place", for they are as near as our daily newspapers.

Springfield is a heck of a town

(State Journal-Register, April 25, 2013)

Thanks to Dave Bakke's indisputable piece of work published April 19, our 25-years-long battle over the home of the Simpsons has finally come to the end.

The Bible says, "then you will know the truth and the truth will set you free." (John 8-32). Now, loser Matt Groening has to eat crow. Rather, he deserves Bart's favorite, "eat my shorts."

After all, Springfield, Ill., is the home of Abe Lincoln, our most favored and famous president, and also it is the culinary home of the legendary horseshoe sandwich. To top it off, we can claim the rightful title of "the home of the Simpsons."

Bravo. Springfield, Ill., wins the triple crowns.

Traditional family still most important

(State Journal-Register, June 13, 2013)

The title of Kathleen Parker's recent column should have been, "The new W-word: Woman" rather than "The new F-word: Father."

Parker's serious question of "why do we need men?" begs a definitive answer: Because the Bible says so.

Genesis 2-18: "Then the Lord said, It is not good for the man to be alone. I will make a helper suitable for him." And 2-24: "For this reason a man will leave his father and mother and be united to his wife and they become one flesh." This is a Judeo-Christian faith upon which our great nation has been founded.

Two scores and eight years ago, I set foot on American soil. Now, looking back, I can hardly believe that our national landscape has undergone a sea change. America is a drastically different country from what we observed in the 1960s; many a thing that was acceptable back then is no longer even permissible or downright illegal.

I often hear people say there are three things that never change – death, tax and change itself. Unfortunately, our traditional family and moral values have steadily declined over the decades. As a result, the divorce rate is skyrocketing, so is the number of single family homes.

Yet, it is comforting to see our respectful seniors in their 80s and 90s stay together. It takes two to tango, so it takes both man and woman to protect and preserve our good old family values.

The unforgettable forgotten Korean War

(State Journal-Register, August 7, 2013)

We just marked the 60ᵗʰ anniversary of the Korean War (1950-53). Still, it is simply unimaginable to hear people talk about it as if it were the Forgotten War.

No one with a pulse would ever forget, let alone overlook the mind-numbing facts that the U.S. sustained the heaviest toll of 37,000 war dead and that well over 7,000 GIs are still listed as missing in action.

The Korean War was almost lost without President Truman's prompt military intervention with his unwavering commitment and determination. It is hard to believe now, but Seoul exchanged hands five times in less than a year, thus the nickname of the "Accordion War."

Also, it is well to remember that the two most unforgettable battles had been chronicled during the war: First and foremost, in September 1950, General Douglas McArthur dramatically pulled off landing at Inchon against all the odds, no parallel of which can still be found in the annals of war.

Second, in the coldest month of December 1950, Chosin Reservoir battle, undoubtedly the fiercest yet bravest of all, took place in North Korea where 15.000 of our allies troops had been almost decimated. This battle may well be the Korean Iwo Jima.

All in all, South Korea owes what she is today to the U.S. and its Allies. To quote George Santanya, "those who do not remember the past are doomed to repeat it."

Boxing causes head injuries, too

(State Journal-Register, Sept 16, 2013)

Football season is upon us. How timely and also commendable it is that high school athletes and their parents are being fully informed about potential head injuries and their late effects from playing football or any other contact sports.

As a matter of fact, there is no better visual demonstration of apparent head injuries than in a boxing match. Any combination of concussion, contusion and actual brain damage does occur when the boxer is down on the ropes, or punch drunken or knocked down for count and finally knocked out. A fatal blow may result in an instant death in the ring.

Chronic Traumatic Encephalopathy ensues as a late sequela. We can cite the legendary Mohammed Ali as a good example. These days, unfortunately, we often happen to watch school kids have vicious physical assaults or fist-fight in classroom and even on school bus. That reminds us of a bare knuckle "boxing match."

As the term pugilistic dementia implies, boxing is considered as the worst villain or culprit of all the contact sports. Some years back, the American Medical Association took its official standing against boxing and, again it is high time to reconsider and accept the AMA recommendation.

Saluting two inspirational lives

(The State Journal-Register, Jan 28, 2014)

What a heart-warming and uplifting story we have in this bitter-cold, dreary winter. I am referring to the recent passing of Jim Solenberger, who was born with the disability of cerebral palsy yet lived his entire life fully and energetically until he breathed his last.

With the deck stacked against him, Jim could earn himself a master's degree in library science and worked 34 years with the Illinois State Library. Literally, he translated disability into ability.

Cerebral palsy is caused by hypoxic-ischemic encephalopathy at birth and its leading cause is prematurity (40-50 percent). It has several different types — the most common being spastic, athetoid/chorea, ataxic, rigidity and mixed types.

Based on my clinical experiences with cerebral palsy patients, athetoid seems to be least affected, or spared mentally, though it may look like a severe case just because of marked dysarthria (inarticulate and mushy speech) and constant worm-like and purposeless movements of the body.

Just like Jim Solenberger, my professional colleague, Dr. Tom Strax, was born with the athetoid CP. He had received his M.D. degree from New York University Medical School and he happens to be a classmate of our prominent local physician Dr. Steve Stone.

Being a physiatrist, Tom finally became the president of the American Academy of Physical Medicine and Rehabilitation a few years ago. In the words of Howard A. Rusk, M.D., my mentor, "Rehabilitation adds years to life and life to years." He went on to say, "Rehab should be everybody's business."

Both Jim and Tom are shining stars of rehabilitation. I salute Jim Solenberger for his victorious and selfless life.

Ban Olympic boxing

(Illinois Times, March 6-12, 2014)

With Super Bowl XLVIII over, people still debate football-related head injuries and brain damage. Recently, President Obama weighed in on the issue, saying, "If I had a son, I would not let him play pro football." Increasing public awareness of harmful sports, particularly among young athletes, is both highly desirable and commendable. Yet, it seems that we are eerily silent about boxing which is considered by far the worst villain and culprit of all the contact-heavy sports. *Pugilistica Dementia* (boxer's dementia) best describes savage boxing for what it is. In light of indisputable medical evidence, it is indeed a sad commentary on the International Olympic Committee that the 2012 Summer London Olympics for the first time ever allowed women boxers (286 of them) to compete in the events in the name of gender equality, thus the London Olympics being called otherwise "women's Olympics."

To quote Dr. John Hardy, a leading neuroscientist and molecular biologist at London Institute of Neurology: "We should not get our fun out of watching people inflict brain damage on each other and having women in a boxing ring is horrible– not because women should not compete alongside men in sports, but because women boxing means more people inflicting more damage on more brains." Hence, it is about time that IOC took some bold action to ban boxing altogether from the upcoming 2016 Olympics.

Progress in genetic testing & counseling

(State Journal-Register. March 27, 2014)

New prenatal DNA blood tests as reported lately are a welcome news to the medical community. They may go a long way toward prevention of some of dreadful genetic disorders, notably Down syndrome (trisomy 21), Edwards syndrome (trisomy 18) and Patau syndrome (trisomy 13).

Furthermore, prenatal blood screening tests are claimed to be by far more accurate and non-invasive as compared with the current methods of amniocentesis and diagnostic ultrasounds. Nevertheless, a tough task rests with the genetic counseling which is part and parcel of preventive measures.

By way of analogy, let me cite two most common and fatal neuromuscular disorders which are also genetically determined and hereditary — Duchenne Muscular Dystrophy (sex-linked recessive) and Spinal Muscular Atrophy, type 1 (autosomal recessive). Both are medically fragile and technology dependent early on.

It is heartbreaking and also exasperating to see one family have two brothers afflicted with Duchenne MD and a sister, though asymptomatic, who is most likely a carrier of the gene, and still another family with two siblings with the same condition of SMA type 1.

It can't be stressed enough that the comprehensive genetic counseling is made available free of charge to suffering families, let alone genetic testing and regular follow-ups, thanks to the Muscular Dystrophy Association. As the old adage goes, "Once burned, twice shy."

Such an unbearable medical challenge in a family naturally exacts a heavy toll on marital relationships. Thus, the remaining spouse, mostly mom, has to carry the heavy burden of being the sole caretaker of her hopelessly sick children. Expert medical advice is one thing and compliance is another.

High hopes for experimental MS drug Lemtrada

(State Journal-Register, June 1, 2014)

I am somewhat compelled to make a brief comment on the May 18 Associated Press article about multiple sclerosis and the experimental drug Lemtrada ("Illinois man lobbying for approval of MS drug that gives him relief").

First and foremost, multiple sclerosis is one of the most baffling autoimmune demyelinating diseases with multifocal lesions or plaques in the central nervous system. Remission and exacerbation are notoriously the hallmark of MS patients, and 60 to 80 percent of them suffer from this type of relapsing and remitting MS. Its clinical course is variable from person to person and totally unpredictable.

Once remission occurs, there is no way of knowing when it will come back or relapse, and with remission phase almost anything or even placebo will work like a "miracle."

Furthermore, MS adversely can be affected by some external factors, such as weather changes, let alone certain underlying medical conditions. Thus, extreme caution is best exercised with evaluation of experimental drugs, particularly for MS patients.

We just hope Lemtrada, though rejected once by FDA, will turn out to be a breakthrough drug upon review. Hope springs eternal.

Head injuries could lead to violence

(State Journal-Register, August 12, 2014)

I am not a strong advocate for corporal punishment, but spanking is needed as a disciplinary measure for children when it is clearly called for.

As the old adage goes, "Spare the rod and spoil the child." Also, the Holy Book admonishes us, "Fathers, do not provoke your children to anger by the way you treat them. Rather, bring them up with the discipline and instruction that comes from the Lord" (Ephesians 6-4).

There is no denying that we live in a violent world and we are plagued with such sickening societal problems as the battered-child syndrome and battered women. But in his commentary Wednesday, "Spanking children: The other domestic violence," John Crisp cited a certain Baltimore football player as a case in point. Further, he alleged that the player's explosive and violent physical assaults as reported against his wife could very well have been caused by the player being once abused as a child. I quote Crisp: "As with most American children, the chances are that someone hit him."

However, as we are well aware, football players and boxers often suffer from chronic and repeated head injuries or chronic traumatic encephalopathy. One of its early clinical manifestations is an unpredictable and uncontrollable outburst of anger and violent behaviors directed toward any person.

Therefore, it seems to be quite a stretch to extrapolate domestic violence from spanking alone.

Jonathan Gluber calls American voters stupid

(SJ-R Nov. 20, 2014)

The people of Illinois were once known as "suckers. But, now American voters are called "stupid", according to MIT economist Jonathan Gluber, architect of ACA. In his infamous videos, the Professor clearly and repeatedly demonstrates his abominable arrogance, the height of which we haven't seen yet. He is also hopelessly bereft of recent shocking history; In 2010 midterm election, voters delivered "shellacking" defeat to the Party in power, thus the loss of House control, and in 2014 election cycle, they "got walloped" according to a Democratic US senator, losing control of both House and Senate

Gruber's disparaging remarks about American voters remind me of Abe Lincoln's famous quote, "You can't fool all of the people all the time,"

US must carefully respond to cyberattack

(State Journal-Register, Dec 31, 2014)

There seems to be a double standard applied to the two huge yet discrete events. One is the 2012 "despicable video," and the other is a recent Sony cyberhacking.

The "reprehensible video maker" was hurriedly thrown into jail, being blamed solely and wholly for triggering the horrific Benghazi attack on the U.S. embassy in Libya. On the other hand, while commenting on the Sony hack, President Obama said, "Sony made a mistake in pulling the movie, and we can't have a society in which some dictator some place starts imposing censorship here in U.S."

Yet the underlying issue of both cases is so monumental as to be constitutional with the First Amendment.

Nevertheless, North Korea's cyber attack is definitely a hostile act. How we respond to such a blatant provocation will determine the fate of incipient cyber warfare.

On foreign policy, Obama detached from reality

(State Journal-Register, Feb 2, 2015)

President Barack Obama's 2015 State of Union speech began with an assertion that the "shadow of crisis has passed."

But actually the shadow of crisis has lengthened.

Terrorism spreads like wildfire all over the globe from Canada to Australia to France, let alone ghastly cruel beheadings of civilian hostages. We have seen the unprecedented rally of 40 world leaders in Paris to protest the Charlie Hebdo attacks.

Radical Islam is, indeed, an existential threat to our society. On the very day Obama delivered the State of the Union message, his much-touted success story with Yemen began to unravel. Rebels seized the presidential palace and forced the U.S.-backed president to resign the following day, throwing the region into a chaotic situation. And Yemen-trained Al Qaeda took responsibility for the Paris attacks.

President Obama has a strong tendency to overestimate his foreign policy while underestimating our sworn enemy. A case in point is his assessment of ISIS as "JV." Obama is so detached from reality that he seems to live in fantasy land.

More information on thoracic outlet syndrome

(State Journal-Register, April 7, 2015)

The March 25 State Journal-Register article, "Back on the bump: Benedictine pitcher resumes throwing after blood-clot surgery," prompted me shed some light on Thoracic Outlet Syndrome.

TOS is basically a neurovascular compression syndrome, involving nerves, arteries and veins, as they pass through narrow passageways leading from the base of the neck to the armpit and arm. There is considerable disagreement about the diagnosis and treatment.

Making the diagnosis of TOS is not easy, because so many other medical conditions mimic it, including cervical disc, fibromyalgia, MS, complex regional pain syndrome, syrinx of the spinal cord and, rarely, Pancoast tumor of the lung, etc.

However, Benedictine pitcher Drake Curry had full-blown, classical signs and symptoms of TOS. There was no way to treat it other than surgical decompression. By the way, TOS is another type of the repetitive strain injuries we often see in baseball pitchers, weightlifters, swimmers and volleyball players, etc. Postural factor is also involved in hyperabduction syndrome with military men.

Most TOS patients will improve with the conservative treatment and physical therapy. But vascular and true neurogenic TOS may require surgery to relieve pressure on the affected nerve and vessel. Chris Young, a major baseball pitcher, underwent surgery for TOS in 2013 and could return to the major leagues for starting rotation.

I hope Drake, as an aspiring pitcher, will have the same surgical outcome as Chris Young had.

Thugs, no matter what you call them

(State Journal-Register, May 11, 2015)

President Barack Obama got it right when he called Baltimore rioters "a handful of criminals and thugs who tore up the place."

The Maryland governor, the Baltimore mayor and the city council president first decried "thugs hurling rocks at police, looting stores and setting fires throughout the city." Then they changed their mind the following day, calling the rioters "misdirected" youths.

That reminds us of one of Shakespeare's famous quotations: "What's in a name? That which we call a rose. By any other name would smell as sweet." And an old Korean saying has it that there is no grave without a reason.

Wind farms detrimental to wildlife

(State Journal-Register, June 6, 2015)

When the feathers hit the fan, it is no longer an euphemistic expression. Rather, it is a serious threat to the ecosystem.

As a part of the clean energy program, wind turbines are increasingly built across the country as a "smart" industry to generate energy, but the unintended consequences are killing birds like a slaughterhouse as they fly into the turbines, particularly during migration.

According to the Wildlife Society Bulletin, it is estimated that wind turbines kill 573,000 birds nationwide each year, including 83,000 hawks, eagles and other raptors. The carnage is much worse for bats with a total of 888,000 annually. Bats are known to use bio-sonar or radar, also known as "echolocating," to hunt for food, including, among other things, mosquitoes.

Yet, wind farms enjoy special treatment, free from prosecution. But this is not how they treat oil or power company when birds drown in waste pits or fry on power lines. It is quite possible, however, that technological innovations will produce less lethal fans and more energy without doubling the number of existing turbines.

Our current wind farms leave much to be desired. We can't help but voice our deep concerns for wildlife, especially endangered and threatened species.

Science behind the mystery of numb feet

(State Journal-Register, June 24, 2015)

In this day and age of modern medicine, we are stunned to read about the "mystery" of a certain case, as in the June 15 article, "Why were my feet numb?"

I specifically am referring to the neurological disorder of Charcot-Marie-Tooth, which also is called hereditary motor and sensory neuropathy or peroneal muscular atrophy. This medical condition, named after French and English physicians in 1886, occurs during adolescence or early adulthood and often is transmitted in autosomal dominant fashion.

CMT has rather distinguishing clinical features of foot deformities, with pes cavus, hammer toes and slowly progressing weakness of both legs, which gives the appearance of an inverted champagne bottle or stork legs. Also. foot drop and a high-stepped gait commonly are observed, with frequent tripping or falls.

CMT's physical hallmarks aside, electromyography and nerve biopsy are the most useful tests for confirmation of the diagnosis. Nerve conduction study reveals marked slowing in conduction, almost down to one half of the normal value. On the other hand, nerve biopsy shows a typical histologic finding of "onion bulb" formation from repeated degeneration and regeneration process. Later in the disease, weakness and muscle atrophy may occur in the hands, resulting in difficulty carrying out fine motor skills.

There is no medical cure, as with any other genetic diseases. But supportive therapy, such as physical therapy, orthotic devices for foot drop and shoe modifications, are necessary measures. Because CMT patients lack sensation, they are prone to develop an indolent ulcer of foot.

As always, the Muscular Dystrophy Clinic provides free comprehensive medical services for CMT patients and their families.

Exercise key to living longer

(State Journal-Register, Aug 3, 2015)

There was a recent study published on the beneficial effects of exercise as related to health issues, such as longevity and obesity. It simply tells us that exercise adds years to our life.

The average 65-year-old can expect an additional 12.7 years of healthy life, meaning he or she will live disability-free until age 77.7 years. Highly active 65-years-olds, however, have an additional 5.7 years of healthy life expectancy until age 83.4.

On the other hand, diet, though a proven and important component of health, is found to be less effective in controlling obesity compared with physical activity. We often hear it said, "You are what you eat," but inactivity rather than overeating could be driving the surge in America's obesity.

Broadly speaking, medicine is divided in three phases: preventive, curative and restorative. If exercise ever came in the form of a capsule or pill, it would literally be a panacea. It is a broad spectrum agent, so to speak, covering all three phases of medicine. Exercise, diet and drugs are readily available to us for good health, and the greatest of these three is exercise or physical activity.

By all means, walk more, get up more and just use your body.

Falls are a major health care problem

(State Journal-Register, Sept 25, 2015)

As we observe fall prevention awareness week sponsored by the National Council on Aging, it is timely to remind the public of some of well-known facts about falls by seniors.

One in three adults aged 65 and older falls each year. Annually, there are at least 258,000 hospital admissions for hip fractures, more than 95 percent of which are caused by falling sideways onto the hip. Women sustain three-quarters of all hip fractures, and white women are more likely to sustain hip fractures than are African-American or Asian women. Osteoporosis plays a major role in this ethnic difference. Naturally, older people are at a higher risk of hip fractures because bones tend to weaken with age. Medications, poor vision and balance problems also make older people more likely to trip and fall.

Between 1996 to 2010, hip fracture rates declined significantly for both men and women. It is unknown what factors contribute to this trend. But by 2030, the number of hip fractures is projected to reach 289,000, an increase of 12 percent. In 2013, the direct medical cost of falls, adjusted for inflation, was $34 billion.

Older adults can prevent falls by doing exercises regularly, focusing on increasing leg strength and improving balance. They should ask their doctors or pharmacists to review their medicine to identify drugs that may cause dizziness or drowsiness, and they should have their eyes checked by an eye doctor at least once a year. They can make their homes safer by reducing tripping hazards, adding grab bars inside and outside the tub and improving the lighting in their homes.

To lower their hip fracture risk, older adults also should get adequate calcium and vitamin D, as well as seek screening and, if needed, treatment for osteoporosis. An ounce of prevention is worth a pound of cure.

Horse-riding therapy has many benefits

(State Journal-Register, Oct 14, 2015)

As a physician, I would like to give my two cents about Hippotherapy and some of the medical conditions that may benefit from it.

The term comes from the Greek word "Hippos," which means horse, and so the literal meaning, "treatment with the help of the horse." Others simply call it "dressage." Hippotherapy is now recognized as a form of medical treatment for conditions like MS, ADD, cerebral palsy, Down syndrome, traumatic brain injuries and other genetic disorders. It has been shown that the natural variable, repetitive and rhythmic movements of a horse offer affected people an excellent platform for improving trunk strength and control, balance, postural endurance and mobility.

During the 2012 presidential election, Ann Romney was ridiculed by the media for riding a horse to deal with her MS. That accusation was made solely out of total ignorance about equestrian therapy having beneficial effects for her. TV celebrity Neil Cavuto is also known to have MS. He is none other than senior vice president of Business News for FNC. He firmly believes that equestrian therapy makes a "legitimate therapy" for MS.

According to Neurology Care and other collaborative studies, some people treated with riding therapy exhibit noticeable improvement in balance, emotional functioning, mood and walking ability. Hippotherapy under the supervision of a trained therapist or instructor can be an ancillary therapeutic modality.

Public deserves truth on Hastert, Benghazi

(State Journal-Register, Nov 15, 2015)

Kudos for the Chicago Tribune's recent editorial, "Public deserves to know truth about Hastert."

Hastert was none other than the longest-serving speaker of the U.S. House and he once held the third-highest elected office in the nation. The issue at stake here is betrayal of public trust.

In another issue of public trust, during the lengthy 11 hours of the Benghazi hearing at select committee, it was finally brought to light that 600 requests for beefed-up security or more protection at the diplomatic outpost were mysteriously all denied. What was also shocking and still puzzling, according to a just obtained email, the former Secretary of State told her daughter on the night of the fatal and tragic event that it was attack by an al-Qaida-like group and that the Ambassador she handpicked was killed along with three communication officers. Furthermore, she also emphatically told the Egyptian president that the attack had nothing to do with the film and was a planed attack – not a protest.

Then why the concocted fable or false narrative, blaming the attack on an anti-Muslim video, which went on for almost two weeks by the Obama administration? Families of the victims were evidently lied to or misled. We also feel they deserve to know about what went wrong with the Benghazi attack.

One more thing; the former secretary flatly denied giving a stand-down order. Then, again, the public deserves to know who gave the order and why.

Sen. Kirk is right about Syrian refugee program

(State Journal-Register, Dec 30, 2015)

U.S. Sen. Mark Kirk is spot on when he called for a pause in the Syrian refugee program, in his recent SJ-R editorial.

Currently, two prevailing yet intricate views on the issue of Syrian refugees are presented to us. One view is espoused by President Barack Obama, in which he would like to compare Syrian refugees to Pilgrims on the Mayflower, "welcoming them with arms wide open." On the other hand, presidential candidate Donald Trump boldly demands a "total and complete shut-down of all Muslims immigration to U.S. until our representatives figure out what is going on."

Unfortunately, both proposals are all unacceptable and extreme under the circumstances. For it is now widely reported that Islam State can make authentic-looking Syrian and Iraqi passports so that their operatives or terrorists can easily infiltrate fleeing refugees. Refugee camps in Europe, particularly France, Belgium, Austria and Turkey are "a hiding place" for Islam terrorists. Furthermore, our background checks system is so flawed that it works like "a sieve." ISIS has become an increasingly serious threat to our national security. We have to pull out all our stops to prevent terrorists from entering the country by posing as refugees. U.S. intelligence Agencies –– FBI, Central Intelligence and Homeland Security –– have their work cut out for them.

ISIS is real, serious threat to America

(State Journal-Register, Jan 31, 2016)

These days, terrorist attacks are ubiquitous, occurring almost every day. Or so it seems.

Yet, President Barack Obama in his last State of Union speech admonished us that "we do not exaggerate the threat from ISIL, lest we play into their hands" and that "ISIL poses no existential threat to U.S."

On Jan. 8, a Philadelphia police officer was ambushed in his car and shot multiple times, but thank God, he miraculously survived the savage attack.

On Jan. 11, ISIS claimed responsibility for four separate suicide attacks in Baghdad and other Iraqi cities, killing 51 people.

On Jan. 12, the day the President delivered his State of Union address, an ISIS suicide bomber in Istanbul, Turkey killed 10 Germans and one Peruvian tourists.

On Jan. 14, two people were killed and 23 injured by an ISIS suicide bomber in Jakarta, Indonesia.

In addition, last month, a God-awful, horrific massacre was carried out by an ISIS husband-wife team in San Bernardino, murdering in cold blood 14 office workers, this being arguably the worst terror attack since 9/11.

How on earth could we possibly maintain our sangfroid with ISIS even getting stronger and more vicious to go after us? Perhaps, we just may have to bury our heads in the sand or follow Philadelphia mayor Jim

Kenney's flat-out denial of reality, "it has nothing to do with being a Muslim or following Islamic faith." One may as well ask the families of San Bernardino victims or the nearly slain Philadelphia police officer whether ISIS is an existential threat or not.

New name is given for chronic fatigue syndrome

(SJ-R 3/20/16)

About a year ago, the Institute of Medicine renamed Chronic fatigue syndrome (CFS) as Systemic Exertion Intolerance Disease (SEID) with its new diagnostic criteria. Systemic implies that the condition affects many body systems, Exertion Intolerance is meant to convey the central feature of the disorder, although most patients are fatigued even at rest, and Disease implies a pathological mechanism underlying the condition, but no disease process has yet been identified.

Take note that it is no longer a syndrome but is considered a discrete disease. The term of Chronic fatigue syndrome was first coined by the Center for Disease Control (CDC) in 1988. However, some people are being cynical about the condition, like "I am always tired and I must have that too". Still others call it a "Yuppie flu" because CFS often occurs after contracting a cold, flu or other viral illness such as infectious mononucleosis. More recently lyme disease is implicated.

New clinical criteria for SEID consists of i) at least 6 months of profound, unexplained fatigue, 2) post-exertional malaise and 3) unrefreshing sleep. On top of that, patients must also exhibit cognitive problem ("brain fog") or orthostatic intolerance, or both. It is now reported that about one million Americans suffer from SEID. Unlike Fibromyalgia, there is no drug therapy available yet.

Currently, many people apply to the Federal Disability Program on the basis of both CFS and Fibromyalgia. We just hope that the new name of SEID will help the medical Community understand better the complex medical condition.

Obama not doing enough to fight terrorism

(State Journal-Register, April 15, 2016)

President Barack Obama told a gathering of religious leaders at Easter prayer breakfast that terrorists want to "weaken our faith" with a pair of recent horrific acts of terrorism in Brussels and Pakistan and cause people to retaliate against them. But he counseled against "succumbing to those particular temptations." He continued on, "If Easter means anything, it is that you don't have to be afraid."

Just two years ago, the president called Islamic terrorists a "JV team." Now, Secretary of State John Kerry in his administration declares Islamic State atrocities genocide. The fact of the matter is that deaths from Islamic terror soared nine-fold on Obama's watch and continues to spread like a wild fire. Any wonder how "JV" turns into genocide. Yet, according to the Wall Street Journal, Obama frequently reminds his staff that terrorism takes far fewer lives than handguns, car accidents and falls in bathtub do. He is even quoted to bluntly say, "They are not coming here to chop our heads off."

It is somewhat troubling that the president himself feels we Americans have an inordinate fear of Islamic terrorism. Perhaps that's the reason why he was doing the wave and tango while Brussels, the center of Europe, was burning. It seems that President Obama is more concerned about Islamophobia than to fight Islamic terrorism tooth and nail.

Pitts' recent commentary off-base

(State Journal-Register, May 16, 2016)

Leonard Pitts' open letter of April 25 was titled, "Sometimes, race is more distraction than explanation." His commentary somehow reminds me of John Fiske of Madison, Wisconsin, and his outlandish and almost delusional idea that AIDS virus was genetically manufactured by Uncle Sam to target black people as a genocidal tool. Back in March 1995, he was even invited by the then-Sangamon State University as a guest speaker on "epidemic ideology."

Yet, the Flint water crisis began almost two years ago when the city changed to the Flint River as its water source. Almost immediately, the city residents complained about discolored and tainted water. The response was, "The water is fine; it's tested and meets all of the health and safety requirements." Thus, the authorities unwittingly endangered the lives of their people, whether young and old, or black and white or rich and poor. Obviously, someone was asleep at the switch.

From my perspective, the Flint water crisis has nothing to do with race and poverty as expounded by Pitts. I quote from his piece, "Granted, there is a discussion to be had about how poverty is constructed in this country; the black poverty is higher than any other with the exception of Native Americans, and that is no coincidence." That is the real issue Pitts should first delve into, rather than spouting off racial demagogues.

We have had the first black president in the White House for almost eight years. No question, black people are by far worse off than any time in recent history. Perhaps Pitts is just tilting at windmills.

Terrorism is the issue, not guns

(State Journal-Register, July 5, 2016)

It seems that political correctness has really permeated our current society. Despite the grisly Orlando massacre perpetrated by another home-grown terrorist, the worst ever since 9/11, we still fail to see radical Islam terrorism as the main villain.

It took six years to redefine the Fort Hood massacre as a terrorist attack rather than shamelessly call it a workplace violence. Fort Hood was the first home-grown terror attack, which occurred on Nov. 5, 2009, less than a year after President Barack Obama took office. We have had our fill of terrorist attacks over the past eight years.

Both San Bernardino and the Orlando massacre six months later are more than enough to convince us that we are at war with Islam terrorism. However, Democrats in Congress are barking up the wrong tree, pulling out all the stops for gun control laws. It is a ludicrous piece of legislation. It is what millennials call a "virtue signaling" to show what a virtuous person they are, rather than actually trying to fix the problem.

Chicago has the nation's strictest gun laws. Nevertheless, Chicago has turned itself into a killing field, like the Wild West. Last year 3,000 people were shot and over the Memorial Day weekend, 69 people were shot, nearly a person an hour.

Where is Congress' outrage? An Islam terrorist may use anything as a weapon, be it a diaper, suicide vest, IED, guns of any type or biological weapon or dirty bomb. We have to bear in mind that what hides behind a gun is a jihadist.

LETTER:
Recent church attack pushes limits

(State Journal-Register, Aug. 3, 2016)

We observe a strange yet discrete phenomenon take place in both Europe and the U.S. Whenever "manmade disaster" hits us, Europeans quickly blame the attack on radical Muslims, whereas we Americans usually grab the terror issue as a prop for strict gun controls. Also, we are agonizingly slow to identify the terrorists as such.

As a case in point, the Fort Hood massacre in November 2009 was attributed to "workplace violence". It took another six years to redefine it as a first major home-grown terror attack. Now, Islamic terror is spreading rapidly across western Europe and America, only getting worse by the day. Last Tuesday, (July 26) two Islamic terrorists killed an 84-year-old priest in Normandy, France by slitting his throat. He was celebrating Roman Catholic Mass at the time.

This was the latest in a recent string of high profile violent attacks in the region that began on July 14, when a radical Islamist drove through throngs of Bastille Day revelers in Nice, France, killing 84 people. No wonder French President Francoise Hollande has already declared a war with ISIS.

This is the first time a church has been attacked amid a wave of terror violence in Europe, signaling the arrival of a type of intimidation long familiar to Christians in the Middle East.

Former French president Nicolas Sarkozy vehemently decried against ISIS, "Our enemy has no taboos, has no limits, has no morals, has no borders. We must be merciless." Pope Francis even said, "The World is at war." But Uncle Sam seems to be rather reticent about the recent gruesome church attack.

LETTER:

Parker not qualified to 'diagnose' Trump

(State Journal-Register. Sept. 5. 2016)

I am compelled to respond to Kathleen Parker's recent commentary, "Trump's head case observations."

To begin with, Charles Krauthammer has both medical and law degrees, and he is also a board-certified psychiatrist. But he didn't imply or even hint in his recent article that Trump's case is compatible with the diagnosis of personality disorder as defined in the Diagnostic and Statistical Manual of Mental Disorders. On the other hand, Parker also wonders if Trump is suffering from some degree of dementia.

However, Parker frankly admits that she herself experienced in the past brain damage sufficient enough to prevent her working for almost a year. In her own words, 26 months after bad falls, she is constantly surprised by incremental improvements after she thought she was well-healed months ago. It is well to remember here that traumatic brain injury is basically different from senile dementia.

Parker wrote that, "while the marketing/branding portion of Trump's 70 year-old brain seems to be as finely tuned as ever, his general behavior insults, diatribes and distortions suggests that some key neurons may have left Trump's tower."

Such a selective control of one's brain is simply not possible with senile dementia, unless he fakes it. Nevertheless, Ben Carson, a world-renowned neurosurgeon and one of Trump's strong supporters, says he is not a regular politician but a businessman, and he tends to shoot straight and does not mince words.

By the way, ages of both the presidential candidates are roughly a year apart.

Bombshell announcement

(SJ-R Nov. 3, 2016)

FBI's bombshell announcement of reopening Hillary Clinton's e-mail scandal, just 11 days before the election, becomes the biggest "earth-shaking" October surprise that we have ever had in the presidential election. It's aftershocks will be felt for a long time on our political system.

This reminds us once again of the old Korean saying, "If you have a long tail, you are bound to be caught after all".

LETTER:

It's morning in America

(State Journal-Register, Nov. 22, 2016, Monday)

I can't help but comment on the Nov. 16 Leonard Pitts column, "It's mourning in America."

Rather, we will shout from the rooftops, "It is morning in America, again!"

We Americans are optimistic because optimism is in our DNA. Pitts, as a syndicated columnist, is clueless and unaware of what has been going on at home and abroad at least for the past five or six years.

About 60 or 70 percent of Americans believe we are on the wrong track, asking for a change of course. I have watched the presidential election for more than 50 years. Granted, the 2016 presidential election was the most divisive and nasty one we've ever seen. All the political pundits and pollsters predicted Hillary's lopsided victory all along, as if it were a done deal.

However, on election night, Mr. Trump pulled off a stunning upset victory. He has won the election fair and square, getting electoral college vote of 306 to Clinton's 232. The American people have spoken. Look at the map, painted red across the United States, except blue smudges on the sides.

Yet, Pitts finds it hard to accept Trump's epic victory. It is, indeed, a pity he remains stuck in his grief stage, ranting and railing against a "white lash." The outcome of the 2016 presidential election reminds us of Abe Lincoln's immortal words: "You can fool all the people some of the time, and some of the people all the time, but you cannot fool all the people all the time."

The truth of Fidel Castro's legacy

(State Journal-Register, Dec. 25, 2016, Saturday)

Fidel Castro's death has triggered a flood of commentary about his legacy. President Obama weighed in and said "History will record and judge the enormous impact of this singular figure on the people and world around him." Donald Trump, by contrast, called Castro a "dictator" and just expressed hope for a "free Cuba".

Nevertheless, one may look no further than Venezuela to know the truth of Fidel Castro's legacy. The late Hugo Chavez had more wholly adopted Castro's economic and ideological model. Now, look at what's happening in Venezuela; Caracas is the world's most violent city and its people are living in abject poverty.

Venezuelans are desperate to leave the country. Where there is socialism, there are always boat people. Furthermore, the average monthly income of Cubans is reportedly $20. We may as well compare this sheer disaster with those Cubans who were lucky or brave enough to flee to America for freedom. Now, they have the largest Hispanic community in Miami and Tampa areas.

Overall, Latinos as ethnic group are hard-working, well educated, and very successful in their pursuit of the American dream. As a result, there are now 30 Hispanics in the House of Representatives and three U.S. Senators. Two of them were strong contenders in the 2016 Republican presidential primary.

Winston Churchill aptly said: "The inherent vice of Capitalism is the unequal sharing of its blessings. The inherent virtue of Socialism is the equal sharing of its miseries."

Remembering our roots

(State Journal-Register, Jan. 28, 2017, Friday)

We had a summer Olympiad in 2016, and Cleveland's Cavaliers did win the NBA title for the first in their franchise history, after being down 3-1 to the Golden State Warriors. But nothing approached the triumph for the Cubs win of the World Series for the first time since 1908. Finally, the Cubs victory was voted top AP sport story of the year.

Speaking of 1908, we are also being reminded of the infamous Springfield race riot, which was sparked by the event that never happened. The shameful event had been swept under the rug, so to speak. But early in 1991, two sixth-graders at Iles School began to dig out for their history project in a statewide competition. What a revelation! They didn't stop there, making a bold move with their petition drive to the city council, lest 1908 should be repeated.

The Good Book says in Luke 12:2: "There is nothing concealed that will not be disclosed, or hidden that will not be made known." Children are eager to learn from adults, but we adults can also learn from children. How could a city that prided itself on being the home of the Great Emancipator also try to run blacks out of their town by brutal force? If this could happen in Springfield, it could happen anywhere in the United States. The idea gave rise to the National Association of Colored People. Therefore, NAACP was born in 1909.

LETTER:

Obama did not bring promise of change

(State Journal-Register, Feb. 7, 2017, Sunday)

Recently, **the State Journal-Register editorialized that Barack Obama** has a "complicated legacy".

Like a messianic leader Obama came into the presidency on a wave of hope and the promises of change.

Barely nine months into office, he was awarded the Nobel Peace prize for "his extraordinary efforts to strengthen international diplomacy and cooperation between the nations." This was a presumptive Nobel price given in high expectations that he would accomplish his ambitious goals. During his acceptance speech, Obama discussed the tensions between war and idea of a "just war," saying "perhaps the most profound issue surrounding my receipt of this prize is the fact that I am the commander in chief of a nation in the midst of two wars."

He tried to keep his campaign promise to reduce America's global involvement, but his willy-nilly retreat led to more chaos. He deposed a Libyan dictator and walked away from the aftermath. His decision to leave Iraq let him claim, "the tide of war is receding" as he ran for re-election, but he lost the House in 2010 and Senate in 2014. Instead, he allowed the Islamic State to gestate in Iraq and Syria as its civil war was burned out of control.

Obama left the world in a mess with floods of refugees and untold human suffering. Obama failed to bring the national unity he promised. Perhaps the most decisive verdict on the Obama era is the sour public mood. Is it any wonder we have Trump as president?

Good news for patients with Duchenne muscular dystrophy

(State Journal-Register, Mar. 27, 2017, Sunday)

What a great news to Duchenne muscular dystrophy patients and their families: The FDA has finally approved defazacort (Emflaza) as a treatment option of DMD for the first time in the U.S.

Deflazacort, like a corticosteroid, works by decreasing inflammation and reducing the activity of the immune system. As a matter of fact, this trial was actually completed back in 1995. More than 20 years later, another clinical trial here showed that among 196 boys with DMD aged 5-15, those kids treated with deflazacort had greater changes in muscle strength with significantly less weight gain than prednisone.

Duchenne muscular dystrophy (DMD) is a rare genetic disorder, caused by an absence of dystrophin, and transmitted by X-linked recessive trait; Boys are always affected and girls are known to be carriers. The first symptoms are usually seen between 3 and 5 years of age and progressively worsen over time. They are usually in a wheelchair by age 12 and most usually don't survive their mid-20s due to life-threatening cardiac and respiratory complications. DMD occurs in about one of 5,000 male infants in the United States and one of every 3,600 male infants worldwide.

Deflazacort does not change the outcome of DMD. However, it helps prolong ambulation, delay wheelhair dependence and reduce the development of scoliosis, thus avoiding its potential surgery, and slows down cardiac and respiratory problems. Speaking from my clinical experiences it is not that rare that we see one family have two or more Duchenne boys, genetic counseling notwithstanding.

My response to Dr. Sunder's letter of March 31, 2017

My comments are made as follows; 1) Any drugs for rare diseases or conditions which affect less than 200.000 in the U.S.A automatically fall under the designation of 1983 Orphan Drug Act. Currently, we have about 12.000 Duchenne muscular dystrophy in the U.S.. Obviously, no big deal. 2) Nowhere did I ever indicate that deflazacort is a miracle drug for DMD. As we all know, there is no miracle drug in medicine. No matter how effective drugs are, they all have side effects, Being a derivative of prednisone, deflazacort is no exception. 3) Marathon pharmaceuticals has never developed nor invented deflazacort. However, they did receive approval from the FDA in Feb. 2017 to sell the drug just because they purchased data from clinical trials conducted in 1990s. Yet, in the middle of March this year, they abruptly sold deflazacort to PTC Therapeutics in the face of the mounting criticism of their "price gouging scheme". 4) Last but not least, I am a retired health professional on the receiving end of health care. Not only am I keenly aware of rising health cost, but also I am much concerned about escalating drug costs. Regrettably, Dr. Sunder makes insinuation that I am a strong advocate for a big Phama company.

Chansoo Kim

LETTER:

Let Obamacare die and move onto other issues

(State Journal-Register, Aug. 1, 2017)

The Affordable Care Act, also known as Obamacare, was conceived in falsehood and delivered in failure.

Former President Barack Obama sold American people a bill of goods by telling lies, including that people would be able to keep their plans and doctors, and that their premiums would go down. Also, Democratic leader Nancy Pelosi chimed by saying lawmakers had to pass Obamacare to see what's in it. Bill Clinton even complained openly about it while campaigning for Hillary last year, saying Obamacare was "the craziest thing in the world" that caused premiums to increase.

The ACA is no longer affordable. Some major insurance carriers have already bailed out on the ACA. But it is amazing to see no one could ever remember now those blatant lies. Furthermore, some Republican senators who voted to repeal Obamacare in the past now have gotten cold feet.

It is also a political truism that once people are given an entitlement, they aren't keen to see it taken away. However, even the stripped-down "skinny health care bill", let alone a replacement bill, all failed in the Senate.

The best option for President Donald Trump is now to simply let Obamacare die on the vine and then move on to the other issues.

LETTER:

More research needed for causes of Alzheimer's

(State Journal-Register, Sept. 1, 2017)

In the Aug. 1 edition in State Journal-Register there was a **heart-warming story.** about a middle-aged man with Down syndrome and Alzheimer's disease, and his much-devoted sister as a caretaker. Down syndrome is well-known to have a strong connection with Alzheimer's disease.

People with Down syndrome are born with an extra copy of chromosome 21 which carries the amyloid precursor protein (APP) gene. Too much APP protein leads to a build-up of protein clumps called beta amyloid plaques and other protein deposits named tau tangles in the brain as usually seen in Alzheimer's dementia. It is estimated that a little over 50 percent of Down syndrome cases will develop dementia due to Alzheimer's as they age. It often appears in their late 40s or early 50s, whereas people in the general population don't usually experience it until they are in their late 60s.

People with Down syndrome, which is sometimes called Trisomy 21, can experience premature aging about 20 to 30 years ahead of people of the same age. It is worthy to note that Down syndrome triggers abnormalities in the immune system, with a higher susceptibility to certain illnesses such as leukemia, seizures, vision problems and heart conditions.

Therefore, basic science research should be vigorously pursued to improve our understanding of the genetic and biological causes of brain abnormalities that lead to Alzheimer's. But sad news: Iceland is reported to be on pace to virtually eliminate Down syndrome through abortion.

Talcum powder is reportedly carcinogenic?

(Oct. 11, 2017— SJ-R)

Johnson-Johnson's Talcum powder has been used safely for ages (since 1893) primarily as a baby skin care product. But out of the clear blue, baby powder now comes under a heavy attack because it is feared to be "carcinogenic".

Recently, a certain law firm hits airwaves nation-wide, claiming that the talcum powder bears a "causal link to ovarian cancer in women". These days, Talcum powder tort cases seem to crawl out of the woodwork. However, scientific, medical and regulatory bodies, including the National Cancer Institute, and CDC opine that" the weight of evidence does not support an association between perineal talc exposure and an increased risk of ovarian cancer. The American Cancer Society also says that there have been "some studies reporting a slightly increased risk and some reporting no increase" Anyway, Too much of a good thing and that for long periods is bound to bring about some serious medical problems. This is also true of many products including soy and coffee, etc.

Furthermore, under the U.S, Supreme Court's Daubert standard, trial judges must consider whether testimony is based on a valid scientific methodology, has been reviewed and is widely accepted within a scientific community. The majority of states in the U.S accept Daubert standard and other states, including California do not honor Daubert.

Any wonder a 63 year old woman with ovarian cancer in Los Angeles was awarded with a $417 million jury verdict against Johnson & Johnson. She claimed she had been using talcum powder for more than 50 years. This verdict is not apparently based on Daubert standard but rather junk science.

Since we live in highly litigious society, frivolous law suits do occur, like the latest example of a couple in South Carolina suing over eclipse glasses.

LETTER:

Comparing Trump to Manson 'over the top'

(State Journal-Register, Nov. 31, 2017)

Calvin Coolidge once said: "The business of America is business."

Did we ever get it right. We have a businessman as our president. But establishment elites obviously hate his guts, going all out to derail the Trump Express train.

Now, Newsweek dares to compare Trump to Charles Manson. This is so over the top.

Nevertheless, how Trump will perform in the Oval Office will help us to deliver a final verdict on his presidency.

Wind farms leave much to be desired

(State Journal-Register, Jan. 7, 2018)

There is increasing concern that energy generation from fossil fuels contributes to climate change and air pollution. In response, governments around the world are encouraging the installation of renewable green energy projects like industrial wind turbines.

Today we have hundreds of these projects stretching across the country, a far greater number of wind farms than we had a decade ago. A few years ago, the SJ-R featured an article about wind farms and their detrimental effects to wildlife, such as the unintended consequence of killing birds as they fly into turbines, particularly during migration.

Recently, the SJ-R featured the Gatehouse Media investigation series which shed light on multiple complaints from people who live or work in close proximity to wind farms. They experience a host of symptoms ranging from sickness, nausea, tinnitus and stress to sleep disturbance, depression and even cognitive dysfunction. These symptoms are apparently caused by a combination of wind turbine noise, vibrations and shadow flicker. Similar medical complaints also have been reported from Canadian wind farms.

This becomes a serious health issue, and more acute as industrial turbines are being placed in close proximity to family homes in order to have access to transmission infrastructure. Yet, some of energy companies dismiss these credible medical complaints as "all bias and not based on facts or science." Finally, wind farms create divided communities on the side.

Our current wind farms leave much to be desired. We can't help voice our concerns for human sufferings, let alone a serious threat to ecosystems.

LETTER:

2018 Winter Olympics

(State Journal-Register, Feb. 9, 2018)

Since the Summer Olympics in 1988, South Korea hosts the Winter Olympics for the first time in Peongchang this month. Understandably, Korean people desire to sponsor the Winter Games enthusiastically with a fanfare like they did in 1988.

Yet, if they believe their first talk with the North in two years helped them to get an agreement from Pyongyang to let their athletes participate, Koreans are dead wrong, judging from the past history.

Certainly, North Korea has always had a sinister ploy to drive a wedge between Seoul and Washington. Pyongyang will never to fail to make hay out of the Winter Olympics. Speaking of the left-leaning Moon Jae-in, in a speech before the National Assembly as president, he called for "a peaceful resolution" to the standoff with Pyongyang over the nuclear weapons program, and said armed conflicts must be avoided under any circumstances."

Now, he frankly acknowledges his policy differences with the U.S., "a concern that we have, a dilemma we face in the current reality." However, in the same breath, Moon also thanks President Trump for helping bring Pyongyang to the negotiation table.

Moon served as chief of staff to President Roh Moo-hyun (2003-2008). His predecessor President Kim Daejung (1998-2003) was Roh's mentor as a pioneer in the "Sunshine Policy." It is in Moon's genes to revive some of Kaesong industrial parks as cash cows for the North. If you have a friend like him, who needs an enemy?

Is it really Obama booming?

State Journal-Register. March. 17 2018

A dyed-in-the wool progressive once said, "Obama before he left office, put U.S. economic policy on "auto pilot". Whatever good or positive changes come henceforth out of it, should be credited to him, not Trump, Is it really Obama booming?

Obama's economic growth for the past 8 years had been dismal with the worst post recession recovery, averaging GDP 2 %, in the meantimes adding up more than 7 trillion dollars to the national debt, and his last year in office saw measly 1.5% GDP growth. Major U.S. companies were steadily moving out of the country with tremendous loss of our jobs. Unemployment skyrocketed particularly among the Blacks and Hispanic people. Part-time employment was new normal rather than the exception. Yet, as usual, former Obama'a Administration economic advisors circled the wagon in an attempt to explain away their boss's pathetic economic record as a product of structural factors rather than policy. For example, Austan Goolsbee, Obama's economic advisor has called Trump's growth goals of 3% GDP "unrealistic" while Larry Summers, Bill Clinton's advisor and former Treasury Secretary declared that "accepting the Trump's forecast of 3% GDP is like believing in "the tooth fairies".

Mr. Summers is also credited with dusting off the concept of secular stagnation and bringing into the mainstream. However, much needed regulatory relief and unprecedented tax reforms are now causing stable growth and better and more jobs. No question, it is a Tump boom. Recent AP polls confirms it.

Tests can be powerful predictors of college performance

(State Journal-Register, Jul. 8, 2018)

The University of Chicago, well-known nationally for its commitment to academic rigor and innovative thinking, now spearheads a movement to drop ACT and SAT scores for admission.

Granted, no test is perfect, but the ACT and SAT have been proven to be powerful predictors of college performance. It is argued that test-optional admission increases diversity, but that claim is highly questionable.

For instance, in South Korea, students taking its version of the college entrance examination can take it once a year. However, ACT and SAT tests allow students to take multiple chances within a year with the hope of improving their test scores. Test-optional admission opens the door for racial preference in the college admission process.

As Attorney General Jeff Sessions recently commented against using race in the admission process, it is "unnecessary, outdated, inconsistent with existing law, or otherwise improper."

LETTER:

Trump has kept his campaign promises

(State Journal-Register, Aug. 13, 2018)

With the news that the U.S. economy grew at a brisk 4.1 percent rate last quarter, all kinds of arcane or even confusing theories seem to crawl out of the woodwork. As a matter of fact, our economic engine has been steadily running along for at least one and a half year with the unemployment rate at record low.

Now one theory is that this growth spurt was possibly due to a "rush" by exporters of soybeans and other products to move their shipments to other countries before Trump's retaliatory tariffs on imports took effect. They say that this sudden jump is not sustainable. Economist Larry Summer tried to explain away with his own "famed secular stagnation" why the U.S. economy could not rise above 2.2 percent doldrums of the Obama years.

However, the Wall Street Journal nailed it down that tax reform and deregulation have finally lifted the economy out of the Obama doldrums. We have to give credit where credit is due. Yet, AP boldly declares, "Trump falsely claims historic turnaround." It is worth recalling that not a single Democrat in Congress voted for tax reform and nearly all of them opposed every vote to repeal Obama's onerous regulations. Had they prevailed we would be still be experiencing secular stagnation.

Angry Americans ditched 227 years of precedent, and for the first time elected a president with no prior political or military experience. However, we elected a businessman president. So far, he has kept his campaign promises.

Media silent on why Palin not at McCain funeral

(State Journal-Register, Sept. 14, 2018)

The late Senator John McCain's funeral services took place recently at the Washington National Cathedral. Both former Presidents Obama and Bush attended the services and delivered their fitting eulogies for the great senator.

The State Journal-Register's front-page headline also declared, "McCain's tributes echo with criticism of Trump." Trump reportedly went golfing Saturday. But the media went eerily silent on John McCain's running mate Sarah Palin being not invited at the funeral services. After all, she was chosen in 2008 to be his running mate, potentially just a heartbeat away from the presidency.

New Drug for ALS approved by FDA

(State Journal— Register Sept. 25, 2018)

Amyotrophic lateral sclerosis (ALS) is a rare progressive disease of unknown etiology that affects the nerve cells in the brain and spinal cord. It is mostly known as Lou Gehrig's disease while in England it is often referred to as Motor neuron disease. The 2014 Ice Bucket Challenge helped ALS raise much needed public awareness along with strong financial support.

The average onset of age is 50-70 years, being slightly more common in men than women. ALS begins with a rapidly progressive weakness of arms and legs with spasticity and fasciculations (muscle twitchings) followed by dreadful bulbar signs of inability to speak and swallow. Death usually occurs from respiratory failure within three to five years from onset of the disease. Recently, the FDA approved Radicava (edaravone) for ALS patients. Mitsubishi Tanabe Pharma developed Radicava for IV injection. The new drug reportedly slowed the decline of physical function by 33%. Needless to say, Radicava falls under the 1983 Orphan drug act.

On the other hand, there is, as yet, no drug available for the Spinal Muscular atrophy (SMA), a childhood equivalent of ALS which is transmitted in autosomal recessive pattern. Both SMA and ALS share one distinctive common feature. They remain highly intellectual or "clear as crystal" though physically helpless. One ALS patient went so far to compare his condition to "living in a glass coffin"

If you have a friend like Moon, who needs an enemy?

(State Journal- Register, October 20, 2018)

When South Korean president Moon Jae-in held the third summit meeting with the North's Kim Jong Un last September, it was rich in symbolism and amity. The North's Kim rolled out the red carpet for Moon. So far, Moon has scored his "biggest success" in his relentless pursuit of his only agenda to integrate the two Koreas economically, thus bringing in a delegation of 200 officials and business leaders to show his commitment. They also issued a joint declaration to hold a ground-breaking ceremony to reconnect rail and road links by the end of the year. They will also work on reopening the Mount Kumkang Tourist Region and Kaesong industrial zone.

On the final day of the summit, Kim took Moon to the symbolic Mt. Paektu. Moon is well known for mounting climbing and he has trekked in the Himalayas at least twice. When they reached the top of the mountain, Moon reportedly declared to Kim." We should write another chapter of history between the North and South by reflecting on the Heaven Lake".

South Korea was once known as a bulwark of Anti-communism, but now it sadly shows a strong affinity for the Kim regime. The majority of Koreans were born in 1953 after the Korean War (1950-53) and the left-leaning Moon was also born in 1953 as the son of North Korean refugees. I said it before, and I will say it again, "If you have a friend like him, who needs an enemy?"

Socialism has no place in America

Posted Feb 20, 2019

With the 2020 U.S. presidential election approaching, the Democratic presidential contenders seem to crawl out of the woodwork these days. Some of the presidential hopefuls not only talk openly about socialism, but others embrace it enthusiastically with open arms.

Here is food for your thought: Winston Churchill brilliantly compared socialism and the capitalism: "The inherent vice of capitalism is the unequal sharing of blessings. The inherent virtue of Socialism is the equal sharing of miseries."

Furthermore, Margaret Thatcher said: "Socialism ends when they run out of other people's money."

President Trump in his recent State of Union speech boldly declared: "America was founded on liberty and independence –– not government coercion, domination, and control. We are born free, and we will stay free. Tonight, we renew our resolve that America will never be a socialist country."

Life and Legacy of My mentor

Howard A. Rusk, M.D. (1901- 1989)

Dr. Howard A. Rusk is known as the father of Rehabilitation Medicine. He termed Rehabilitation Medicine as the "third phase of medicine" following "Preventive medicine" and "Curative medicine and surgery". It is the period when the "fever is down and the stitches are out". By the means of rehabilitation he used to say we also add "life to years and years to life". He firmly believed that a person did not "need physical wholeness to be the best at a particular occupation whether it be lawyer, doctor, elevator operator, teacher, researcher, potato peeler or even the President of the United States." He also stressed that rehabilitation should be "everybody's business". Come to think of it, the word "Rehab" is nowadays ubiquitous.

Dr. Rusk was born on April 9, 1901 in Brookfield, Missouri. As he later wrote in his autobiography, the town was "about half way between Hannibal and St. Joseph-or halfway between the worlds of Mark Twain and Jesse James". Rusk was the son of Michael and Augusta Shipp Rusk. At the age of eleven, Howard became interested in medicine. A local physician agreed to let Howard serve as his assistant, watch him perform surgeries, and go on house calls in exchange for cleaning surgical instruments. In school, he "wasn't a great student-just a bit above average". After graduating from high school, Rusk enrolled at the University of Missouri in 1921. During his second year of college, his family was hit by the Depression. Rusk's father told him that he should leave school and get a job to support his family, but his mother would not allow her son to drop out of college. He remained in school and worked two jobs to pay for his education.

Rusk's interest in helping the disabled began when he joined a college fraternity, Phi Delta Theta. One of the fraternity's staff members was an amputee who "thumped around on crutches, trying to do his work". Rusk and his fraternity brothers raised money to buy the man a prosthetic leg. Rusk remembered, "I can still see his face when we presented it to him. That leg meant everything to him, but it also meant a lot to me because it made me feel the crucial importance to a handicapped person of something the rest of us took for granted-ability to walk".

In 1923, Rusk received his bachelor's degree from the University of Missouri and subsequently earned his medical degree from the University of Pennsylvania School of Medicine. He married his college sweetheart, Gladys Houx, on October 20, 1926. Rusk spent the early years of his career practicing medicine and teaching at Washington University Medical School in St. Louis.

During World War II, Rusk joined the U.S. Army Air Corps (now U.S. Air Force) and was appointed chief of medical services at Jefferson Barracks in St. Louis. Rusk noticed that wounded and disabled servicemen were left to "simply lie around getting custodial care, with nothing to do, bored to distraction, helpless, waiting for some kind of infection or disease to carry them away".

Life and Legacy of My mentor

Rusk later recalled, "gradually the concept of rehabilitation came to me as I found out how much really could be done for these men. In the beginning, I knew only that every thing possible should be done to return them to physical and mental health. This meant finding ways for them to function despite their disabilities." In other words, the idea of rehabilitation was conceived during his medical services to the U.S. Army. It was really born out of sheer medical necessity.

Rusk developed a rehabilitative program that helped wounded and disabled servicemen return to military duty and, eventually, civilian life.

When the war ended, Rusk wanted to continue to help the disabled even though some members of the medical community thought he was wasting his time and, in fact, they considered his idea of rehabilitation "RUSK's Folly". At this point, Rusk went to New York to further consider the NYU position. While in New York, he discussed his career options with a number of prominent New Yorkers with whom he had become acquainted while in the military. Among others, Arthur Sulzberger, owner and publisher of The New York Times, suffered from severe arthritis and was sympathetic to the plight of others with disabilities. He invited Rusk to write a weekly column to help raise awareness about rehabilitative medicine. Financial support from wealthy and influential individuals such as financier Bernard Baruch and businessman Bernard Gimbel and his wife, Alva, helped Rusk establish the Institute of Physical Medicine and Rehabilitation at New York University in 1950. This center is now known as the Howard A. Rusk Institute of Rehabilitation Medicine.

Stroke victims, amputees, people paralyzed after contracting polio or suffering an accident, and individuals born with birth defects were among the many patients who sought out Dr. Rusk and his staff for treatment. One of his most famous patients was Roy Campanella, catcher for the

Brooklyn Dodgers. One day in 1958, he was driving home and his car overturned on a slippery road. He fractured his 5th cervical vertebra and severed his spinal cord, thus becoming a quadriplegic patient. However, he was turned into W/C independence from rehab, at the Rusk Institute.

Another famous patient was Joseph Kennedy, father of President Kennedy, who suffered a devastating stoke in late 1961. After the tragedy, the family asked Dr. Rusk to go down to Florida for consultation. He helped set up a rehabilitation program for him, first at the hospital, then at his home in Palm Beach. Finally, Kennedy was admitted to Rusk's Institute for further Rehab.

Working tirelessly to help others, Dr. Rusk founded the World Rehabilitation Fund (WRP) in 1955 to help people with disabilities in underdeveloped countries around the world. The WRP continues to help people today through its work in countries such as Cambodia, Sierra Leone, Afghanistan, and Lebanon.

Recognized as an expert in his field, Rusk served as a consultant to nine U.S. presidents (from Truman on down), the veteran's Administration, and the United Nations. For his work and achievements, Rusk received many awards and honors. He had received altogether sixteen honorary degrees both in the United States and abroad. In 1974, the University of Missouri named its rehabilitation center in honor of Rusk. Rusk was also nominated for Nobel Peace Prize, but did not win.

"A World To Care For", the Autobiography of Howard A. Rusk, M.D.

In 1972, Rusk published his autobiography in which he described in details what he did to develop and spread the concept of rehabilitation in the U. S. and throughout the world. This book is a must-read for all physicians, particularly physiatrists (specialists in Rehabilitation Medicine). I made it a policy for all my staff to read Rusk's autobiography for a review of its history. Following the Annual PM&R convention in 1973 in Washington D.C., we had a gathering of NYU Alumni at the Washington Press Club and Dr. Rusk appeared there, announcing the publication of his autobiography. I was thrilled to receive his autographed copy "For Dr. Chansoo Kim with friendship, Howard A. Rusk 1973."

1) Dr. Rusk had been president and chairman of the Board of the American-Korean Foundation since 1953. He took it over from Dr. Milton Eisenhower.

2) Dr. Rusk suggested "an isoniazid saturation campaign" for Korea in 1953.

3) A Korean boy named Tong II Han was sent to the United States.

4) Henry Betts, the director of the Institute of Rehabilitation at Northwestern University in Chicago.

5) President Truman once asked Dr. Rusk, "Howard, have you ever had to fire God?"

September 4, 1969

Windsor C. Cutting, M.D., Dean
University of Hawaii – School of Medicine
Leahi Hospital
3675 Kilauea Avenue
Honolulu, Hawaii 96816

Dear Doctor Cutting:

I am very happy to inform you that I have decided to accept the appointment as Associate Professor and Medical Specialist of Physiatry in Okinawa.

May I assure you that, as a member of the University of Hawaii faculty, I will under no circumstances fail to abide by the regulations of the University of Hawaii Postgraduate Medical Education Program.

I am confident that my forthcoming assignment in Okinawa will be challenging and one of the more rewarding experiences in my career.

At the present time we feel that we will be able to travel to Okinawa via Honolulu in the latter part of December. Immediately following my wife's confinement, I will notify you of our date of departure so that the necessary travel and shipping orders may be issued at the military headquarters in Hawaii.

I appreciate very much your affording me an opportunity to serve with your faculty.

Sincerely yours,
Chansoo Kim, M.D.

My most unforgettable professional colleagues — Dr. N.L. Gault, Jr and Dr. Sarah Gault

One of Dr. Gault's most remarkable contributions to International Medical Education was the pivotal role he played between 1954-1961 in the development of Seoul National University (SNU). The wonderful eulogy of Dr. Jung-Gi Im, the then-dean of SNU, described Dr. Gault's leadership in restoring SNU College of Medicine to it's world prominence today. At the celebration for the 50th Anniversary of the U of M/SNU Partnership, they hosted a dinner in recognition of Dr. Neal Gault. He was obviously loved and greatly respected by them. A $60,000 check was donated to the International Medical Education and Research Program of the University of Minnesota Medical School. On the other hand, Dr. Sarah Gault built the first department of PMR at Okinawa Central Hospital practically from the ground up. She diligently took care of local stroke and spinal cord injured patients while teaching the nursing staff how to take care of them. During last two years of her tour in Okinawa, she made her department fully operational and functional with the staff of reserved Navy Lieutenant physical therapist, a local Okinawan physical therapist, one OT and one carpenter. Simple ADL's devices such as commodes, walkers, canes were constructed with locally available plastic pipes by the hired carpenter and issued them to their patients free of charge. I found her to be extremely competent and talented as well as compassionate. I still remember her personal story back in 1954, when they stayed at The Bando Hotel, the only Western-style available to them. One day, their baby son, John, fell down from the crib because of faulty side rails, and received a bloody nose and how their children suffered from parasite infestation they got from the hired local house girls. Sarah was also kind and generous enough to share with her personal experiences living in Okinawa for the past two years. She felt somewhat uneasy about my two young children, warning me with "motherly concern", "Don't let your kids ever play in the sugar cane fields. There lurks highly a poisonous snake Habu." Sarah was a kind of person who "grins and bears it".

My Role as Physiatrist In The Department Of Physical Medicine and Rehabilitation at OCH (1969-1971)

Sarah Gault M.D., a physiatrist, was the founder of the department of PM&R at OCH. (1967-1969). She did a yeoman's job in making the department fully functional and operational with adequate staff, when I stepped as her successor.

In addition to taking care of acute stroke patients on the ward, we had received many requests for lectures and Rehab. In-service workshops from local hospitals and the Koza Nursing School, the Crippled Children Hospital and Naha General Hospital.

In February 1970, we conducted a four-day workshop for the Government of Ryukyu Islands nurses at Miyako Hospital and Nanseien Leprosarium, medical facilities located on Miyako Islands, 178 miles southwest of Okinawa. This was in response to a request from the medical institutions to the U.S. Civil Administration of Ryukyus (USCAR). It was such a long, bumpy and stomach churning trip by helicopter. But the visit on Miyako was the time well spent. We were delighted by the interest, cooperation and enthusiasm of the participants.

The workshop team consisted of myself, Dr. Chansoo Kim, Physiatrist, Betty Lawson, RPT, Miss Sumiko Hanna, nurse consultant, Miss Yoko Tokorodani, all from the University of Hawaii Advisory Group at the Okinawa Central Hospital, Captain Clifford Pennell, registered physiotherapist, US Army Hospital, Camp Kue, Miss Myrtle Konna, public health nurse, USCAR's HEW Department.

In May 1970, the same team conducted another workshop at Yaeyama offshore Islands which is near Formosa.

Since the introduction into PM&R Department of an Electromyography (EMG) in September, I received the largest number of EMG consultations, 16 cases altogether. EMG consultations were requested from other hospitals, namely US Army hospital at Camp Kue and Crippled Children Hospital in Naha.

Dr. Ooghe (UH Pediatrician) and I used to drive down to the Crippled Children Hospital in Naha once a month as consultants usually with a trainee of OCH.

I often had to fill in as a Neurologist. There was no neurologist on the UH staff at the time. The whole GRI staff by now became fully aware that Electrodiagnostic test (EMG) was readily available to them. Therefore, it was expected that the number of EMG consultations would continue to rise as time passed. As a case in point, Dr. Yamada at the Crippled Children's Hospital in Naha requested EMG for two cases of Muscular Dystrophy and one case of Myotonia congenita which is a very rare case. This Myotonia congenita was such a classical case from the electromyographic view point and the case was subsequently published in the Hawaii State medical journal upon my return to Hawaii.

Conclusion

1) At the end of his tour of duty in Okinawa in 1971, Dr. Kim received a meritorious citation from OCH.
The citation is as follows.

"Since your arrival in December 1969 as Associate Professor of PM&R with the University of Hawaii School of Medicine Postgraduate Medical Education Program, you have devoted yourself enthusiastically to the teaching of staff doctors, trainees and nurses by providing excellent lectures and invaluable clinical instruction concerning early care of physically disabled persons caused by injuries and diseases. You have contributed much to the elevation of medical standards and total rehabilitation of patients.

Upon your departure, the staff of Okinawa Central Hospital wish to express our gratitude and at the same time and wish you and your family good health and much success in the future . March 11,1971. Joji Arakaki ,Director of OCH, Government of Ryukyus."

2) The Office of High Commissioner requested that we conduct Rehab. workshops for offshore local hospitals in Miyako and Yaeyama, 178 miles, Southwest of Okinawa. High Commissioner Lieutenant General was interested in Rehab, as part of his Civilian Projects for Okinawa. Workshop team consisted of myself, as Dr. Chansoo Kim, Physiatrist, Betty Lawson, registered physical therapist, Sumiko Hanna, Nurse Consultant, Captain Clifford Pennel, registered physical therapist, US

Army Hospital, Camp Kue, Miss Myrtle Kanna, Public health nurse, USCAR HEW Department.

3) EMG was first introduced to Okinawa with the help of USCAR.

4) Dr. Kim obtained his medical license to practice in Okinawa.

5) The only picture in the book shows Dean Gault, University of Minnesota Medical School met with my father and my father-in law in Taegu. The meeting was arranged by my Uncle, Chae Won Kim, Professor and Associate Dean of Medical School of Yonse University. Later, Dean Gault, told me that he had the most delicious Japanese meal he ever tasted," better than what he had in Japan".

6) Okinawa was reverted to Japan in June 1971 as one of their Prefectures.

Printed in the United States
By Bookmasters